# Random Thoughts on Life & Love

*For Thom & Paula from Debbie*

*By Judy Sevec*

*Love, Judy Sevec*

# Rapier
## PUBLISHING COMPANY

# Random Thoughts on Life & Love

Copyright © 2022 Judy Sevec

ISBN 978-1-946683-43-4
Library of Congress Control Number 2022900846

Rapier Publishing Company
Dothan, Alabama 36301

www.rapierpublishing.com
Facebook: www.rapierpublishing@gmail.com
Twitter: rapierpublishing@rapierpub

Book Cover Design: Syed S. Zaidi
Book Layout: Rapture Graphics

Rapier
PUBLISHING COMPANY

# Dedication

I dedicate this book to a wonderful Priest from Ireland,
Father Patrick Gallagher.
Thank you for your dedication and devotion.
You have been such a blessing to me and so many others.
God Bless you always, dear Father Gallagher

Love Judy Sevec

# Acknowledgements

First, I want to thank God for giving me life and love, and the ability to write about it all!

I want to thank my friend, Joyce Corcione, without her, my book would never have been written. I showed her some of my poems and she typed some of them for me. While we were talking on the phone one evening, she told me she had read some of the poems to another friend of hers and her friend thought they were good. I had thrown my notebook of poems in a corner, collecting dust. Well, I got them out and decided to pursue my dream of writing a book of poems.

I want to thank my husband, Tony, who has encouraged me so very much and helped me keep the faith. He constantly tells me, "You can do this, you can do it. You can make your book happen." He has read and edited some of my poems and always encourages me to carry on!

I want to thank my Publisher, Rapier Publishing Company, Fannie A. Pierce, my hero, such a strong, sincere, and Christian woman. I met her a few years ago at the public library, where she was teaching a class about publishing a book. She is even ex-military, which is impressive. She's an author and an advocate to help victims of human trafficking. She went above and beyond to assist in making my book a reality.

# Table of Contents

# Random Thoughts

# Chapter 1

## God, Faith, & Hope

## REAL

Jesus, Jesus be real to me
Jesus, Jesus, with me be
Jesus, let me touch your face
Jesus, I know you died in my place
Jesus, Jesus, be real to me
Jesus, I want you to live in my heart
Jesus, I really want a new start
Jesus, Jesus be real to me
Jesus, I long to hear your voice
Amid all my daily chores and noise
Jesus be with me at morn and at end of day Jesus in my
heart always stay!

## FORGIVEN

Let us all live as we should
Always striving to do good
Jesus is the one to follow
You will see
This is how it's meant to be
Jesus is my heart
My path He will chart
Though, we're far from perfect
We can be forgiven
And by His grace go to Heaven

## ANSWERED PRAYER

In the name of the Father, Son,
And the Holy Spirit
I longed to be Catholic and
Now I belong.
I'm glad, God you did listen
And bring me along.
All the ceremonies
All the old traditions
And also the adoration
Peaceful times of meditation.
Jesus, Mother Mary, and all the Saints
I pray for their help to direct
My paths.
And I have the Father to
Lead the way
A shiny example of love
Day after day.

## BLESS MY SOUL

Bless my soul Oh Father Dear
Bless my soul, banish my fear
Forgive my sins in Jesus' Name
Bless my soul and touch my heart
I must be saved and do my part
I should go to Mass everyday
I hunger to hear every word You say
Bless my soul
Make me feel whole

## TRADITIONS

Incense and candles, traditions, and more
Catholic Church – Your Spirit will soar
"Upon this Rock I'll build
My Church," He said so long ago
Read the Bible and you will know
Vestments for different days
Different colors, Royal Purple,
White, Green, Red, lead the way
Worn by a Priest, looking so regal
By whom we've long been led
They bless the altar and anoint
The sick, baptize, and wed
And always on call
And Mass every day
It's universal…they lead the way

## MY PARISH PRIEST

Man of Devotion
He's seen every emotion
He's there for the mighty
And there for the least
No need is too large
Or there's no need too small
If you need Him, He will come
No matter, early morn, or dead of night
He will come to make it right
Always a twinkle in his eye
Always gives comfort to those who cry
With his own special style and smile
For folks, he'll go the extra mile.
With Irish wit and wisdom
He brings souls to the
Heavenly Kingdom

## DEAR MARY

Dear Mary intercede for me
Dear Mary your love I can see
Your love I can feel
To me you are so real
Dear Mary, precious dove
Mother of all, we feel your love
Your beauty is so ethereal
Your loyal answer to the call
Dear Mary, I'll pray the rosary
As I've been taught
As my salvation Jesus bought
Holy Mother of us all
On you we can always call
I Love you Mary and
Always will
You calm my spirit and
Keep me still

## MEN IN BLACK

Our men in black
So strong and admired
From the Seminary to the altar
They never falter
They are trained and taught and blessed
They're very busy, not much rest
But you can always know
These spirit-filled men are the best.
Their days start early
And can end late
But all their flock thinks
They are great.
We feel they are ours
And they are so devoted
And have given us so many hours.
Men in Black, a special club
Strong, smart, spiritual, and examples of God's love.

## ANGELS

Angels, mighty and beautiful creatures have
always been around
Their wings make a beautiful sound.
To me they seem shy, yet strong
To Guardian angels they belong
Angel Gabriel, the famous and wise
Beautiful sights in the skies.
They dwell among the wispy clouds
But also among us, have no doubt.
On the walls of the Vatican in Rome
I see this as an ancient home.
They fly with the birds as beautiful spirits in the sky so blue
They were always here I always knew.
And with thoughts of them my spirit renews!

## THE SKY

I look at the sky and see the face of God
In the blue and the pink
And the fluffy white clouds
Look at the sky and you will see
How beautiful Heaven will be
The Fluffy White Clouds
Forming silhouettes
Drifting by
They look iridescent
Surrounded in pink against
The deep blue sky
I can't wait to be there and fly
With the angels on gossamer wings
To be totally immersed in Holy things
Heaven will be so glorious
He gave us the sky just to see
How gorgeous our home will be.
And sometimes He tosses out a rainbow
Just to give us a show
In the sky I always see the
Face of God and His Son
When I sit on the grass
And gaze at our brilliant sun
I always remember the Holy One.

## MORE THAN GOLD

I learned the lessons of life late
I didn't even realize that God is Great.
But the Catholic Church has saved my life.
Holy Catholic Church, the Love of my Life.
Life in the Eucharist
Love and Commandments
Love for Christ
God, Holy Spirit and Sacraments.
You've refreshed my spirit
And saved my soul
Our Heavenly Father, worth
More than Gold!

## ST. FRANCES

I love horses and I love dogs
But cats are precious as can be
Birds are the best and
Mean the most to me.
St. Frances is my Patron Saint
He was all about faith and love
So he was very blessed from above.
He loved Jesus, people and all
The animals too.
He was very brave and true.
Dear St. Frances, Heaven is blessed
To have you there with all the rest.
Saints and angels up above
Awesome Holiness
Peace and love.

## HOLY MARY

And then one day we will meet
Mary, chosen to be Jesus' Mother
Above all others.
Virgin Mary so perfect and pure
It had to be her for sure
Virgin Mary, come to me
Virgin Mary, pray for me.
Holy Mary, Mother of God
If we ask she will pray for us
If we just ask and trust.
She is all Love
Like a gentle dove
So pray the Rosary every day
Say to her Thank You
And help me and pray and pray!
Always love Mary, Jesus' Mother
Always love Mary, she's like no other.

## COPPER PENNIES

Copper pennies we must count
We are poor without a doubt
Not much money but plenty of love
We do have blessings from above.
When we are poor, we must scramble
To pay the bills and get a handle
We empty out our piggy bank
As we realize our fortunes sank
We need help and so we pray
And pennies from Heaven
Fall our way
Thank you, Thank you, God above
You are all Mercy, Grace, and Love
Thank you for the pennies from above
And always thank you for your Love!

## LOOK UP

Where did the time go?
Where's my rainbow?
There's been plenty of clouds & rain
But I know we must look
Beyond the sorrow and pain
Oh, I've had sunshine too
It's just today my mood is blue
We all know in this life
We must, at times cope with strife
But when times are good or bad
When we're happy or we're sad
Upon the Lord we must depend
Look up to the Lord and all
Prayers send!
To your needs He will attend
Believe these words for they
Are true
So keep the faith that's
What to do

## COME HOLY SPIRIT

Come & from the start
Please come & live in my heart
Come & always stay
Come & tell me what to say
Holy Spirit I Love your light
In the Chapel I've felt your might
You really are a moving Force
You lead us all to make a choice
You nudge us in the Direction we must go
From Heaven your Spirit flows
Holy Spirit help us to spread the Word
Pope Francis says, "Evangelize, let the message be heard."

## SPREAD THE WORD

Believe, believe, you must believe
Read the Bible and you will see
You will see how life should be
You will see how we should be
Read and know how good Jesus is
And you will want your life
To be like His
Turn your life over to Him now
And your life will matter,
He'll show you how
We all have gifts, use for good
Spread the Word as we should
Spread the Word, near and far
Shine your light like a
Shining star

## "STUMBLE"

Wish I could be a better person.
Really wish I could be a better person.
But I always stumble and fall.
Then oh, Lord back to you I crawl.
We all want to turn our backs on sin.
But there it is, again and again.
So, to be better, I'll continue to try.
I'll just try to be better y'all,
Even though I may fall.

## UPS AND DOWNS

Oh, what a world we live in
It's a world of ups and downs
What a world we live in
I know, I've been around
They say when the world gives you
Lemons make lemonade
I agree that you can do it,
Just don't be afraid
I've had highs so high
I felt giddy
Then lows so low I was
Filled with self-pity
But we pull ourselves up and
Then we pray
And God always hear us
No matter what we say.
God can lift us from so low.
Our God is a God of Grace,
Amazing grace that will always Flow.

## COME HOLY SPIRIT

Come Holy Spirit come
Dwell within our heart
Come Holy Spirit our path to chart
Come Holy Spirit strengthen us
Our ally to be.
Holy Spirit comfort us
When the way we cannot see
We need you, Holy Spirit
To dwell within us
We know your help we can always trust
Sent from God through Pentecost
Sent to help save the lost
Sent from God, our help and comfort
Here on Earth
Sent to help us always to put God first.

## "THE PRAYER MEETING"

This Mother Hubbard doesn't live in no shoe
This Ms. Hubbard the Bible she knew.
She must have read it from cover to cover
She's a Real Bible lover
She taught us really well
We now know all about Heaven and Hell.
She's an inspiration
In a weary nation
We get together every week
All of us the truth we seek
We love each other
And Ms. Hubbard
We all look forward to each Monday
After we go to church on Sunday
Then we have our sweet prayer meeting
Getting together with hearty greetings.
We'll delve deep, we won't give up.
We'll boost each other and raise prayers up!

## SHOW ME

If you love me show me
If you love me show your love
If you love me look above
No faith without deeds
So go where I lead
Use our talents to do good works
Use our treasures to tithe,
You know what's that worth
And our time, use wisely to
Worship and help others
Do what's expected and go the mile further
God will reward you
You know that's true
He will be pleased by the
Good deeds you do
Show our love to all we know
And you will see how much Your happiness will grow!

## READING THE BIBLE

I picked up the Bible
And just began to read
I've been reading the Bible
Not even knowing where it would lead.
I love to read a Psalm
I really find it makes me feel calm.
I love to read the Bible
Before I go to bed
I love the words in red,
The words that Jesus said!
This is a habit that I love
I find inspiration from above
When I dwell on the Word
My prayers are heard.

## "MY ANGEL"

Have you seen my angel?
Long time, no see
How can this be?
I missed you, but you went away
I have missed you every day.
I waited and waited
I looked and looked
But alas, you were gone
And I was so alone
Will you return to me?
Or is this never to be?
I won't give up, I can cope.
I think I'll never give up hope.
Come back, angel, come back to me.
Ours is a love that was meant to be.

## LOVE OF LORD

I love my Lord
I ask for His mercy.
I love my Lord
For His Word, I'm thirsty
I love you Lord
With all my might
Let me never lose Sight
Of your glorious Light.
Light of the world, Glorious and Bright
You light the world on the darkest of nights
We must also be lights of the world
And carry our flame
We must let everyone know your name!

## HOLY MEAL

I really love the Eucharist
It makes me cry
I know that God is here
I know that God is real
Takes away all fear
Lord's Supper is a Holy meal
Yes, I love the Eucharist
I pray that God will hear
I pray He'll know just how I feel
I know that He is alive and real
Holy, Holy, Holy meal.

## IF ONLY

If only I could have been a nun
Can you imagine the fulfillment you get from serving the Son?
I saw all the movies, had all the daydreams
Was always in awe
Of the dedication I saw
Why did I not follow through?
Why, with everything I knew.
It's sad it seems
I could've lived those dreams
I could have changed my life, and so many others
I could have taken my daydreams so much further
But I went a different path
It was not to be
Only much later
We look back and see.

## BROTHERS & SISTERS

Brothers and sisters, we are all
Brothers and sisters, the great and small
Brothers and sisters, regardless of color
Brothers and sisters, we love one another
Brothers and sisters in good times or bad
Brothers and sisters happy or sad
Brothers and sisters, we'll always be
Brothers and sisters from sea to sea
Brothers and sisters in Christ, the whole human race
Created in love and saved by grace.

## END OF DAY

Monday, A.M., and my alarm clock
Is screaming at me
Lots of places I have to be
Hurry and scurry and run
In circles
Rush to and fro and jump
All the hurdles
Go from early morn until evening
Sometimes I wonder what's the meaning?
Then my Day's done and I go to the Chapel
And feel the Presence of my Lord
I kneel in the Sacred Silence thinking
Of His Word
I revel in the silence of This Holy Place
I kneel and pray and still in silence, just – be
And His Peace washes over me

# I HEARD A VOICE

One Eve I Heard a Voice
As clear as it could be
I heard this voice say to me
"You may not have long to live"
The voice was real and made me
Think – I must learn how to give.
I think of what I heard every day
And I know I have a debt to pay
So many blessings have been given to me
I must give back, find a way
So every day I pray
Lord show me the way
Show me what I can do
Little ol' me what can I do?
Lead me Lord, take my hand
Lead me Lord, give me a plan
A way to help in your name
Not to make a difference would be a shame
I do not have long to live, I'm old
Teach me Lord in your name to be BOLD!

## TRY

I love you Lord with all my heart,
I loved you Lord from the start.
I know my Lord loves me
And I love Him
But I should be more devoted
Wish I went to Mass every day
Why am I selfish and go my own way?
I know I could be better
I know I should be good
I wish I lived as I should
I know if I tried I could

## COME BACK

I've been heart broken, but you
Can come back
Believe me…It's a long way
But you can get back on track
I've been down so low that the way back
Was very slow
But when you get back to the land of the living
You raise your hands
And you are again…believing

## CAN YOU IMAGINE?

Can you imagine being a nun?
When I was young growing up,
there were so many movies
With nuns so devoted.
Their devotion and happiness I noted.
Do you remember Deloris Hart?
She left behind Elvis, fame, and movies to become a nun
Cause' she felt the call within her heart.
Movies with Catholic schools and nuns
Made a deep impression on me.
As a young girl, I could see
The nuns had so much devotion, purpose, and peace.
Only the Lord, they had to please.
These movies from my youth I never forgot.
And later, I joined the Catholic Church, married a Catholic –
look back? Not!
Every priest and nun I've met, you can see
In their life – peace and joy beyond compare.
The peace they have can you imagine?
Imagine?

## BACK TO CHURCH

We were away for a while
Then we came back
Back to the fold, with love and smiles
We came back for the Eucharist,
A sermon, and songs
We really had been gone too long.
This church is my heart
It hurt to be apart
Here our spirit and soul are fed
This is truly where we are led
Our great priest is so dear
He brings in the Eucharist, our Savior so near
We had the virus and now we are healed
We received a blessing as we came and kneeled
Thank the Lord that we came back
Back to the fold
Where we belong
And thank Father Jim, for his love
And for his sermons so strong!

## FAITH

Faith is something we're
Blessed to have in our life
If we didn't have it
How could we deal with strife?
Don't you always call on Him
When your need is great?
You always call on Him,
Before it's too late.
He's our friend in need
He's our best friend indeed!

Random Thoughts

# Chapter 2

Happy, Glad, & My Favorite Things

## FAVORITES

Fresh cut grass
Or after the rain
Snow along the coast of Maine
Favorite things that lift my spirits
Rainbows and puppies and kittens
Or standing by the fireplace
And warming my mittens
I love the orange & golden leaves of fall
And to hear the brisk wind and the Eagles call
I love Central Park covered in snow
Or warm and green or by lamplights aglow
Christmas in Dixie
Walks on the beach
Swinging on the front porch
Many favorites within our reach

## ADVENTURES

My hubby and I got married at Seville
Our love has always been real
Then to New Orleans we went
That's where our honeymoon we spent
Then also we went to the beach
Nothing seemed beyond our reach
We even went to Hawaii
What a special treat
We went there with his family to meet
We went to Graceland, home of the King
The sweet famous star who could really sing
We love to go to Apalachicola, Florida often
A great little village to relax
We always want to go back
My favorite trip was to my favorite city NYC!
The city that never sleeps
These memories we'll always keep
Memories & Love so deep

## I LOVE NYC

I love New York City,
The city that never sleeps
I love New York City
She is in my heart for keeps
It's a city of lights
A city so bright
I love New York City and Central Park
Covered in snow,
It's the whole world's park
I love New York City and Times Square
Times Square, it's a jewel so rare
Ellis Island and the Statue of Liberty,
People came from everywhere
The dream of Liberty to share

## FLOWERS

Lavender and roses
Colors, colors, sights to see
Tulips and posies
Flowers are pretty to me
Pink, red, yellow, all
Beautiful petals, large or small
God's creation
What a palette
Every color, tone, and tint
Flowers feed the soul
In their rainbow colors
Flowers are always given by lovers
And they bring love and light
Yes, bouquets are a welcome sight
So, bring one to someone right away
And you know you will brighten their day!

## OLD FRIENDS

There's nothing like the long-time friends
There's ups and downs and in-between
They know all about your faults and flaws
But they still love you "just because."
Old time friends share memories that go so far back
And old-time friends will always "have your back."
The friends you've known so long
They really know where you belong
They can even give you good advice
Because they even know you need to be nice
So, get back in line
And they can share their precious time
It's never too early or never too late
To call up the old friends and make a date.

## DOWNTOWN

I love downtown or our town, whatever you call it
I love the traffic & the lights,
Even the people who come out at night
I love the cafes and the avenues
All the city-scrapes and views.
I love the people all walking around
Like only you can do downtown
I love downtown what a special place
I love downtown, it's the heart of my city
I love downtown, to me it's all pretty!

## NOSTALGIC

It was fall, that wonderful time of the year,
and nostalgia abounds.
Colors of fall all surround
Oranges, yellows, and browns.
There's a chill in the air
And we all know it's
Time for the fair
We'll eat candy apples
And pumpkin pie
We'll carve jack-o-lanterns
And build bonfires
I delight in it all
My favorite time of year
The season I hold most dear
My glorious colorful fall!
My dear Lord, the colors
Of your palette are the loveliest
In my sweet fall!

## LONG & SWEET

There's a Love between Husband and Wife
It's a Love to last all their life
They came together and made a vow
They'll love each other as only they know how
Each one's different but the love is the same
Their love is there whether or not
Their's is fortune or fame
They carry on side by side
They're both along for the long wild ride
And if they're blessed it will be long
As the theme of a beautiful Song
Long & Sweet
With a deep & meaningful beat

## FRIENDS

How many friends do you have?
You can never have too many, you know
Be blessed with friends and thank the Lord each time you pray
Thank you, thank you, Lord I say,
Thank you for each friend that I have, everyone & all
On any one I could call
It's great to have good friends, y'all!

## THE COFFEE SHOP

I love to sit at the coffee shop
At the eve of my busy day when it's time to stop
I see the young people with their "young" talk,
all with backpacks and books
And their trendy looks
They talk and giggle and flirt
Each girl wears a sweater and a mini skirt
They all have computers and books,
and seem to study and write
They're an interesting and lively sight
So relaxing, coffee aroma fills the air
What a cozy and comfy lair
Sofas, booths, and overstuffed chairs
Their world seems so secure
The best time of their life for sure
It's a great way to end my day
For a couple of hours always I enjoy
The coffee and atmosphere
It takes me from stress to another sphere

## "CHRISTMAS IS COMING"

Christmas is coming
It's snowing outside
There's hustle and bustle
And presents to buy.
Santa and his elves are busy
Building toys for all the good
Little girls and boys
A fire roars in the fireplace
The dining room table is covered with lace
And a smile shines on every face
Tonight, we'll go to Midnight Mass
And experience the happiness this Holiday has
Beautiful Mass with glowing candles
And flowers all to honor the Christ child
And His dear Mother, so sweet and mild
Jesus has come hallelujah, our Savior was born
It's a glorious Christmas morn

## MELODIES

Music and melodies sooth the soul
Or awake the senses
All the way from rock and roll
Music really gets us moving
Sometimes it gets us "grooving"
We love the sound that a trumpet has
Yeah, we really love all that jazz!
From voices in the choir
To concerts on the stage
Where the new songs are all the rage
Babies love lullabies
They sooth them if they cry
At church, we love our songs
About the sweet bye and bye
Some like old-time gospel
And some like rhythm and blues
Those old songs about love we could lose
So, turn it up and let it be
Whatever tune brings you joy and glee!

## "TRUE LOVE"

Love, true love is a blessing from God
Marriage is a sacrament sent from above
Listen to God and He will lead
Marriage is not for two, but three
Include God in your marriage and together pray
Listen to what I say
It will only get better if you obey the Lord
Then you'll be of one accord
2 can be 1 as it is God's will
And trust in your union with joy
He'll fill
So, honor each other and put God first
As a married couple, you'll flourish!

## THE THIRSTY PIG

And then we went to "The Thirsty Pig"
Cutest little pub you've ever seen
Bar-B-Que & Tacos abound
And on the patio, a band will sound
It's in Alabama
So you know, Southern hospitality flows
It's a real laid-back place
Lazy & relaxing, no such thing as haste
So come & stay a little while
With family and friends
And enjoy and smile
Kick back & just stay a longer while

## MY FRIEND JOYCE

I have a friend named Joyce
She tells it like it is
But she's a witness for the Lord
For she's a friend of His
She reads her Bible everyday
Everyday what she does is pray
Each day in the eve
She's on the phone
With a dear friend
Reading Bible verses
As their day comes to an end
All her love and support she'll lend
I love Joyce and she loves me
It's good to have a friend like her
I can call and she'll pray for me
And I feel blessed as can be!

# WINTER!

Don't you just Love Winter & Fall
Some folks like Halloween best of all!
I love the cold weather & big heavy winter coats
Flannel, wool, and cashmere
I really wish it would snow down here
But snow down South, the chance is slight
But we're happy when it comes
What a beautiful sight!
We dance around and take photos galore
Because it may be years before we get any more
But I love all the sights and aromas of Winter and Fall
Halloween- all orange and black and contest at the mall
Thanksgiving – cook a Turkey, large or small
Then Christmas – red and green and some
of the prettiest decorations
You've ever seen
Winter so many reasons to love this season!

## TRIP

We love to go to a parade
And to the fair, take the Ferris wheel for a spin
Even to a concert now and then
You gotta go and you got to do
And even go on a trip or two
Let's make the most of the time we have
Let's live it up when we can
The more we can see
And the more we can do
Is just a plus along the way
Try to enjoy most every day!

## DAYDREAMS

I wish we lived in New York City
The City that never sleeps
I would love to live there for keeps
We, so far, only went once but it was great
I hope we go again before it's too late
In my daydreams, it's where we live
When I lay my head on my pillow at night
Daydreams swirl
And we're walking the streets filled with lights
Then we walk in Central Park
We love this city that never goes dark
Wow – Daydreams are a Lark!

# Random Thoughts

# Chapter 3

## Very Lovable Are All God's Creatures

## LOYAL PETS

I love dogs, cats and birds too
My love for them is nothing new
I always knew how precious they were
They're loving and loyal and true
If you want a friend who will love you so much
You must have a pet to feel this special touch
You love them with all your heart
And they've loved you back from the very start
Go to a shelter and adopt if you can
I did this once and what a friend!
When we got home, she ran under the bed
She didn't know yet what a great home she had
This little kitty loved me so –
Her favorite place was in my lap
Where she loved to purr and take a nap

## HOW MANY CATS

How many cats do you have?
We have 4, let's see
Two are my kitties
Two are his
3 inside & 1 in the yard
And now we have a newcomer here
But what can we do?
Where did he come from – where?
This is how cat people are
One is never enough
Even tho' to care for them all is rough
We love them one & all
Sometimes they come when you call
They're all so loving & sweet
We have to get them off the street
I know round the house there's so much fur
But it's worth it when you hear them purr

# BIRDS

From the mighty eagle to the smallest wren
Birds are very special, always have been
On Eagles wings I wish I could fly
I'd fly beyond the deep blue sky
Birds like angels can fly high
What beautiful creatures, winged
What beautiful songs they sing
I love cardinals & blue jays too
Parakeets I've had a few
But my Quaker Parrot
Was my favorite one of all.
He could sing and dance
Strut around so tall
He was so smart
And he was my heart!

# JADE

We had a bird named Jade
We loved him from the start with all our heart
He was so beautiful and smart
Jade would dance and he would sing
On his little rope he would swing
I taught him to kiss and wave
Fed him every treat he could crave
Jade was pretty, bright green
Prettiest bird I've ever seen
We were so blessed to have Jade
Thank God for this blessing you made
We'll never forget him
We had him for twenty years
He was so very dear.

## CATS AND KITTENS

Cats and kittens
Gloves or mittens?
We love the animals, big or small
We love the animals, care for them all
Cats and kittens are so sweet
I always have a kitty laying at my feet
Or have a kitty curled up in my lap
They love to stalk, run, and play
But most of the time, it's nap, nap, nap
You feel so good when they purr
'Cause you know they know they're loved for sure

## THE "SITTER"

Sometimes I "baby sit" for dogs
Their owners call me when they go away
And I'm glad to come and stay.
I love doggies and they love me.
There's not one, but three.
I sit in the back yard, and they run and play.
Then we come in and on the rug we lay.
Then at night we sleep on the big, big bed.
I wake up in the morn to licks and kisses all over my head.

# Random Thoughts

# Chapter 4

## Memories:
## Rustic & Relic, Happy & Sad

## MUSTY MEMORIES

I sat in the musty attic and opened
The heavy lid of the dusty old trunk
And memories come rushing out
Memories, memories of what I'm all about
So many memories, some good, some sweet
And some so sad
Good times we had
But some rush in and hurt so bad
This trunk was stored away so long ago
Before I knew the path I'd ever go
I ran my fingers over the old music box
The first gift he ever gave me
Tears filled my eyes
Some feelings never die
Then I saw the promise ring
It made me smile
Promises we kept only for awhile
There's the quilt my mother made
I never wanted it to fade
Lots of old photos, faded, and cracked
If only I could go back

## MY BROTHER & ME

When we grew up, my brother and me
I think we were spoiled as could be
Our mother was poor & worked
So hard to give us all she could
We know now that she spent more
Than she should
We left that little town
Where we grew up so long ago,
Went here & there & all around
Now we live close by each other
So, that's a blessing we live near by
Just down the road, over the hill,
And just a few miles down the road

## SHORT WHILE

We're only here for a short while
I hope we can make many, many
People smile
Otherwise, why are we here?
It's our calling, to others, bring joy and cheer
Testify, spread the Word
Be loud and proud
Make sure you are heard
Be inspired and let it show
When you are called… never say no
When you are called… always go
Go to the depths and back
Never, never get off track
We must all go many a mile
We are only here for a
Short, short, while

## HOPSCOTCH

I remember hopscotch,
As a child I loved to play.
Hopscotch was fun as a little girl.
It was fun to pass the time away.
I think I'll play again,
Take chalk to my sidewalk.
I bet someone will stop and play with me.
Someone walking down the sidewalk will turn 'round,
Come back and play with me!
Take me back to a simpler time.
A time that's left so far behind.

## THE PAST

An old Blue willow plate & coffee cup
But the dishes are chipped
And the sets all broken up
The lace on the table is yellow with age
Turn, turn, turn the page
We lost our innocence long ago
Now just dust and cobwebs grow
The quilts of many colors have faded
And now you know I feel old and jaded
The old iron skillet is rusty now
It sits – black and empty, I wonder why?
No table is set, no "bring the extra chairs"
And now it seems – no one cares
I can blow the ashes out of the old fireplace
I can still feel the warmth on my face
Relics of the past, a past so near
Yet so far away
You know I feel so moody and gray
Sad to see so much fade away

## PERFECTION

Round and round I go
Faster and faster, I go
Then all at once I was knocked to my knees
And a future I could not see
Like I was left out in the cold
Almost like I had no soul
I look in the mirror and who do I see
Who is that old reflection?
Looking back at me?
That image in the mirror can't be me
In my mind I'm young,
I can't be old
Have all my songs been sung?
Have all my stories already been told?
But I know the Lord can save my soul
I know there's a better place to go

## TIME OF OUR LIFE

I remember the times of our life.
I remember the friends of our life.
Do you remember too?
Tales we told were true.
Friends are scattered near and far.
Some are close, some afar.
Some wrapped up in another life
Some gone on to the afterlife.
I hope to see them all again
In spirit form we may be,
But still my friends I will see
I feel the Twilight closing in
But that's alright
Look where we've been!

## EMPTY SPACE

Today is his birthday
But he passed away
Still, it's his birthday
And all I can do is say,
I miss him so
Why did he have to go?
My dear, dear friend
With whom I spent time
My dearest friend
So sweet and kind
There's no one to take his place
My heart will always have
An empty space
My time with him was filled
With fun and laughter
I did not know sadness
Would come after
Heaven has a new bright star
But his passing left many a scar
I miss him every day
Memories of our time will come
And never fade away

## ANOTHER DAY

Another day has come and gone
It went by so fast
Another day has come and gone
Why can't the good days last?
Another day, month, another year goes by
And we all see how fast the time does fly
As a child, it took the longest time
One Christmas to another
For me and my little brother
Oft times I wonder how many days
Do I have left
Sometimes I wish I could
Go back and always I wish
The good times would last

## COPE

I've lost love and I've lost friends
I hardly know where I've been
And wonder how it all will end
It's been a wild ride,
Try to take it all in stride
But…sometimes I just want
To run and hide
Now I try to face the future
Full of hope
Deeply felt hope that with it all,
I can cope
I must always have hope

## MY DAD DIED

My father died today-
I feel so sad
What can I do,
The things I should have said.
My dad died today
I feel so sad he's gone
How can I make up for
Things I could have done
I pray the Lord will help me
I pray he'll lead the way
For me to come to terms
That he's gone away today.
I know he's not gone far
I know that he is near
I feel him looking after me
So that I have none to fear.
Tonight's so very sad
Where did time go?
I wish I could go back in time and say,
"I love you so!"

## MY DEAR FRIEND

My friend is sick…
He has M.S.
I don't believe his fate is sealed
I pray every day he is healed
What a shock, so young and full
Of charm
How could he ever come to harm?
He's loved by so many,
His troubles were few
But now…learning about
A disease we never knew
So now I look up and kneel
Down and pray everyday
Also, ask others to please
Please, please pray!

## DARK TONITE

It's dark outside
And dark in my heart
I want to crawl Inside my shell
Do I need a new start… a new story to tell
My mood is dark and sad
Like the black sky outside
Too many regrets I've had
What or who could turn the tide?
Come Holy Spirit and give
Me peace
Erase my sins
I fall to my knees
God, God forgive me please

## DON'T WORRY

Don't be anxious He said
Your life has gone where I've led
Don't worry, now or then
Just pray and pray and don't sin
Don't be discouraged or lose hope
Whatever happens, with me
You can cope
I will be by your side
Just look to Heaven and
Keep my Spirit inside
Your life is planned
You are in my care
So don't worry or fret
For my plans for you are set
Keep the faith and know
You are in my hands
So be patient and know
For I have a plan

## MY SECRET GARDEN

Sometimes I look around and see darkness and despair
Sometimes I see that does not seem fair
So, oft times in the evening I like to slip away, so
My cat and I away we go
Along beside the gray stone wall,
where the wild pink roses grow
The tall trees form a canopy, where as a child I used to play
And now I often come to pray
My cat and me we stay for hours
Basking in the fragrance of all the wildflowers
Here I pray for peace in the world
Here in this place, I know my prayers are heard
Mother Mary comes to me
As I clasp in my hands my Rosary
I caress the beads and recite my prayers
And the Spirit of my Father envelops me there
I love this place where I feel God's grace
And I'm so very glad it's in a secret place
And now the eve is slipping away-
But cat and me, we want to stay

## SENIOR - TIME

Now my appointments are all doctors
Now there's shots and x-rays and tests galore.
Then there's diagnosis
And the prayer soars
There's fear and sometimes tears, medicine and tonics,
So many things seem ironic
They say what goes around, comes around,
I find that to be true, the good and the bad,
There's enough to go around or so I've found.
But there's trust and hope for a better place,
A much better place at the end of the race.

## "WHERE'S MY AMERICA?"

I hardly recognize America anymore.
She's changed so much from shore to shore
They took prayers out of the schools
And now they wonder when violence rules
My America, what happened to you?
Turning back to God is what I pray you'll do
Is it too late? Can you turn around?
Listen to God and the way can be found.

## COME TOGETHER

I love America, Land of the free
I pray we can turn back to God
Before we have to flee
So much chaos & so many riots
But God can take us to new heights
We must come together & we must pray
That's the main thing we must say
Black, white, yellow, brown, or red
We must all calm down & pray
Thank God we live in a land
That's free – That's what I say
I think we all care about each other
We think about each other as sisters & brothers
God, we pray, we Love you, Thank you,
Keep us free! Please let it be!

## MS. FLO

I met a lady, Ms. Flo.
She was in her nineties at the time,
but spunky as could be.
She was very special to me.
She wore the cutest little shoes
And always a long skirt.
She always joked around,
And said she was "old as dirt."
She prayed for her America every day.
We all should be like her and pray and pray.
Lord, keep America a Land of Freedom,
Until we all go to your Heavenly Kingdom.

## IT'S ALMOST OVER

It's almost over 'cause
I'm so old
Time went by so fast just like
I'd been told.
For my sins I must atone
Spread peace and Love
Cause soon I'll be gone
I know many friends who are alone
I'll call them up and for hours we're on the phone
We relate and really enjoy our talks
Then some days we go for walks.
And now for this eve my Bible I've read
And now I think
I'll go to bed....

Random Thoughts

# Chapter 5

## Just Thinking…Freefalling

## HOW MANY ANGELS

How many angels did you see today?
Guardian angels show the way
But also, many other angels you will see
Friends when you need them there, they'll be
There are angels to lead the way
They'll come to you especially when you pray
They're so close, so near by
They're here and also on High
Thank God for angels everyday
They're here to help in every way!

## MAKE A LIST

Make a list
And do it now
Make a list
Do it how?
I really make too many lists to do
Then I accomplish way too few
I'm really good at making lists,
Just not too good at carrying through
What, oh what can I do?

## AGELESS

I have a friend who's 88 years old
How does he stay so blessed and bold?
He had a hard start in life,
But maybe it was a blessing, after all
Cause he grew up to be so tall,
Not in statue, but in his life and all
He has a family who adores him
I'm so glad for them
He has a strong faith
God bless him and his family too
You know he will be there for you
Being so faithful and true

## HAVE MERCY

Lord, I am so busy
Running to and fro
But what does it amount to
If I lose my soul?
I need to slow down
And talk to you more
For I know in my heart
When you knock at the door.
Lord, help your people in
These days of chaos
For you are the only one
Who can help us?
My church doors are open
Such a place of solace and peace
I'm glad the doors are open
We pray God have mercy please.

## I CAME BACK

And then I turned away
But I came back
I really knew all along, I knew the way
The way is still straight and narrow
But that's ok
Go this route and
You will find the way
And when your time here is done
You'll find it was all worth it
It was more than fun
It was an amazing run
God planned it all from the start
He put Jesus in our heart

## READY?

He will come back again
Will we be ready?
Yes, He will come back
Always be faithful & steady
He may come back soon
And He will banish the chaos and gloom
If we go with Him to Heaven above
All we'll know is goodness & love
There on the clouds we may fly
Like gentle doves & angels in the sky
If only we've been saved from sin
We can fly to Heaven – when?
Are we forgiven & ready to go?
I really, really hope so!

## MUSIC

Sing a song for your soul
Music can sometimes make you whole
Gospel music is really great
The lyrics will speak to your heart
Listen to music when you are down
Because your sorrows you can drown
Music can sooth & it can heal
Sometimes no matter how you feel
The strum of a guitar
The beat of a drum
Listen, listen & the emotions will come
Can you write or sing a song?
Cause if you can you'll belong
Listen, listen
Turn your ear & you will hear
Play a good & mellow tune in your head
And you'll have a good day
Listen to these tunes as you go along your way today!

# HURRY

Help me, help me, Lord I pray
I pray to my Lord every day
I know that I'm blessed
Forgive me Lord because
Sometimes I just feel sad
I'm not mad, just sad
Although I try
Sometimes I just sit and cry
I pray to my Lord
Give me peace
My dear Lord, shut off all the worry
I'm sorry for my sin
Please, please help me again
Turn off the worry
Lord, help me – hurry, hurry
Stop all the worry
Hurry – Hurry

## IN JESUS NAME

Thank you, thank you God for
Giving us the gift of your Son
Thank you for Jesus, the Chosen One
How could we express the
Gratitude that we feel
Tho, we will always pray and kneel
Jesus, Jesus, the Precious One
Jesus, Jesus, the Chosen one
What a plan you had when He came
Now we always pray, "In Jesus name."
It's always the same
In Jesus name!

## CLOSE FRIEND

It's so good to have a close friend
It means the world to me
Cherish each & everyone
I know you're blessed as can be
For every close friend you can see
See each one as a gift from above
A gift born out of love
A special gift from above
Because between close friends
It's all about love, love, love
Love for each other to keep you strong
Love for each other like a soulful song
Love that will last so very long.

## BLESSINGS

How many blessings do you have?
Count each one
How many blessings do you have?
Each one came from the Son.
Son of God gave His life for you
If it was only you, He would have done it
If it was only you, it would have been the same
If it was only you, He still would have come!
So, think about it
Count all your blessings
They come from above
They are formed out of Love
Count your blessings
Don't take for granted all of this
Be thankful and grateful
And of your blessings make a list

Random Thoughts
Some Big & Some Small

"Random Thoughts
On Life & Love"

Random Thoughts
From Sad to Glad

Random Thoughts
All From Above

About the Author

First time author Judy Sevec was born in Pensacola, Florida. She lived between Florida and Alabama. She worked for many years as a waitress, and her love for people and adventures made her job very rewarding. She met her husband of twenty-eight years, Tony through a dear friend. Tony is a Catholic, and she became Catholic. She and Tony reside in Dothan, Alabama. Coming out of retirement, she now works as an In-House Service assistant for seniors. Through this, she has met many interesting and inspiring seniors.

As an avid reader and dreamer, one of her passions was writing. She never stopped believing that one day she would become an author. Now, after many years of believing, the dream has come to fruition. Her first book, *"Random Thoughts on Life & Love"* is a compilation of beautiful thoughts she encountered throughout her life. She says that if anyone enjoys her book, she will be happy.

CPSIA information can be obtained
at www.ICGtesting.com
Printed in the USA
JSHW060157031222
34248JS00007B/141